Let's Find Out About
Ice Cream

by Mary Ebeltoft Reid • Photographs by John Williams

LET'S FIND OUT
LIBRARY

Scholastic Inc.

New York   Toronto   London   Auckland   Sydney

We are grateful to Ben & Jerry's® for the opportunity to
photograph this book at their Waterbury, Vermont, factory,
and especially to Lee Holden for his generous support.

Photographs by John Williams
Illustrations by Ellen Joy Sasaki
Design by Alleycat Design

1   2   3   4   5   6   7   8   9   10   02   01   00   99   98   97   96

I love ice cream!
Where does it come
from? Let's find out!

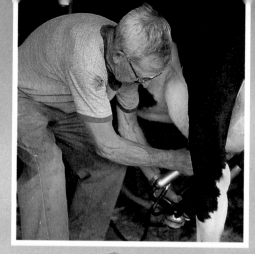

Ice cream comes from cows' milk and cream.

It takes a lot of milk and cream to make ice cream.

HOMOGENIZED
KIM MILK
(1.89L)

ARTHUR TILLEY/FPG

HENRYK T. KAISER/ENVISION

Sugar from sugar cane plants
is added to make it sweet.

There are chickens' eggs
in ice cream, too.

At the factory, a mixologist blends everything together to make the ice cream mix.

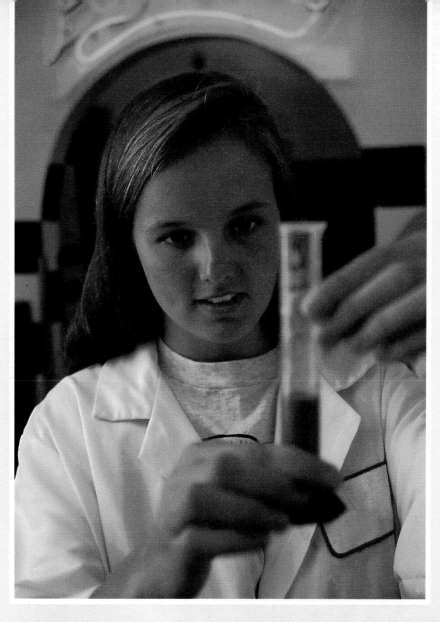

The mix is heated. Then a scientist tests the mix.
She makes sure it is healthy to eat.

Pumps push the mix through pipes and into tanks.

Next comes the flavoring.
This batch will be coffee flavor!

**The mix is still soupy. Inside this freezer it gets harder.
Then when the chunks go in, they won't sink.**

Now come the chunks. What would you like? Chocolate? Candy? Berries? Nuts?

13

The ice cream is almost ready!
Machines pour it into containers.

Other machines wrap 8 containers together in plastic. Then they go into the spiral freezer.

Inside the spiral freezer the ice cream gets really hard. Then it rolls into a very cold warehouse. The warehouse workers wear freezer suits!

These people check orders and put the ice cream into trucks.

Freezer trucks take
the ice cream to stores.

It's time to make more ice cream! A worker cleans the machines with a big hose. Then everybody starts a new batch.

Flavorologists invent new ice cream flavors!
Testers taste ice cream every hour.

They make sure it tastes good. Aren't you glad they do?

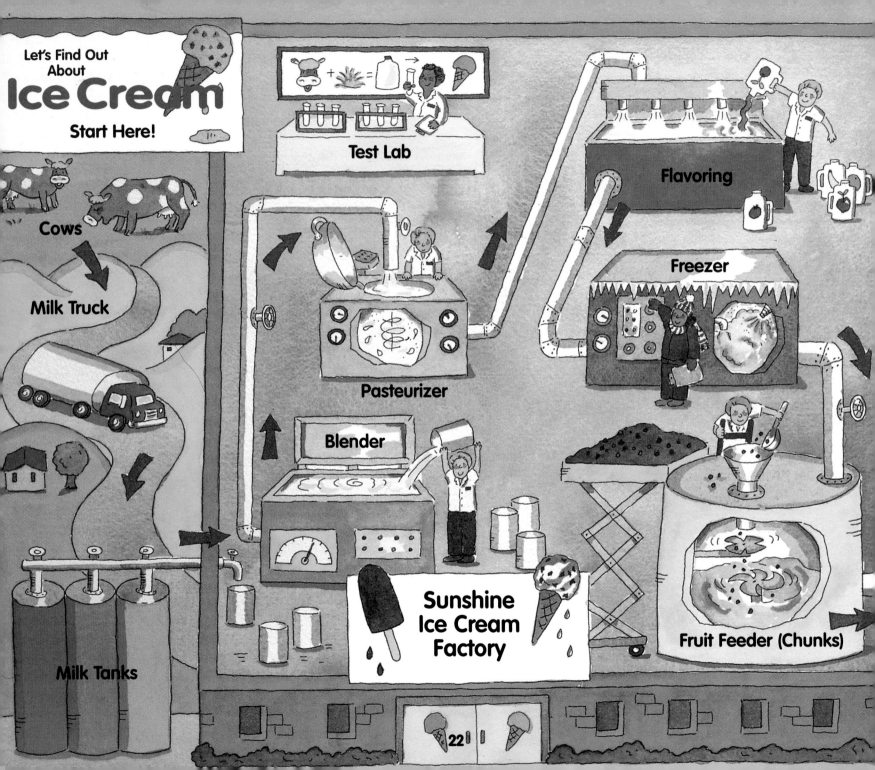

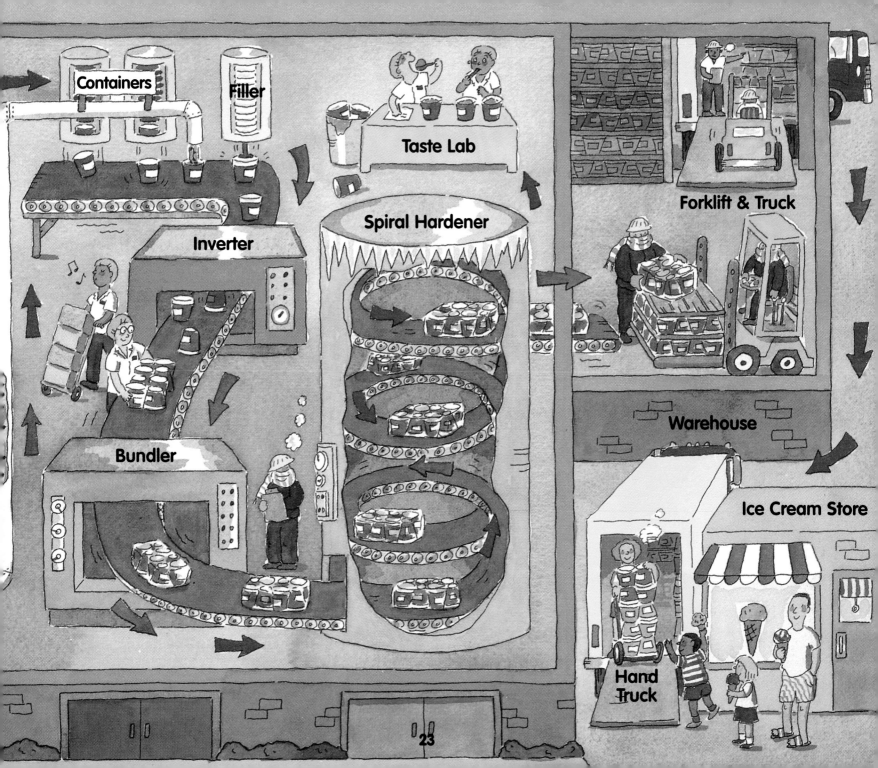

Containers

Filler

Taste Lab

Forklift & Truck

Inverter

Spiral Hardener

Warehouse

Bundler

Ice Cream Store

Hand Truck

23

For Grown-Ups

We hope you have fun with this book! Here are some things to do as you read and enjoy it together.

Before reading, talk about favorite kinds of ice cream and ask, "Where do you think ice cream comes from? What is it made of?" Children may enjoy reviewing (and revising!) their guesses after reading.

Read and reread!

Read once through the whole story. Then reread, taking time to look closely at each picture and talk about it.

Retell the sequence of ice cream making. Use the illustration on pages 22-23 to help you tell the story.

Talk about the jobs the workers do, and the clothes and equipment they use.

Be the machines! Dramatize the sounds and actions of machines such as the mixers, the filler, the bundler, and a forklift.